A. J. Carnes

A. J. Carnes' Manual on Opening and Closing the Books of Joint Stock Companies

A Work Designed fo Experienced Book-Keepers. Second Edition

A. J. Carnes

A. J. Carnes' Manual on Opening and Closing the Books of Joint Stock Companies
A Work Designed fo Experienced Book-Keepers. Second Edition

ISBN/EAN: 9783337061128

Printed in Europe, USA, Canada, Australia, Japan

Cover: Foto ©Andreas Hilbeck / pixelio.de

More available books at **www.hansebooks.com**

A. J. CARNES' MANUAL

ON

OPENING AND CLOSING

THE

Books of Joint Stock Companies.

A Work Designed for Experienced Book-keepers.

ILLUSTRATING THE
VARIOUS METHODS OF OPENING THE
BOOKS OF JOINT STOCK COMPANIES, WHOSE ORGANIZA-
TIONS ARE PECULIAR, TREATING WITH NOMINAL AND FICTITIOUS
VALUES; THEIR DISPOSITION AND THEIR USES; HOW AND WHEN THEY
SHOULD BE USED, ETC.; EMBRACING PRACTICAL INFORMATION TO
THOSE BOOK-KEEPERS WHOSE EDUCATION HAS BEEN
WITHIN THE CONFINES OF THE COMMON
COMMERCIAL COUNTING-ROOM.

PRICE, $3.00

SECOND EDITION,

BALTIMORE, MD.

1888.

DEDICATED

TO

HON. ODEN BOWIE,

EX-GOVERNOR OF

MARYLAND.

Whose ability in the management of large corporations of which he is at the head, is greatly admired.

BY THE AUTHOR.

To My Fellow-Craftsmen.

THE nature of Joint Stock Concerns in their organization is varied and often peculiar, owing to which the opening entries at the commencement of business must necessarily differ, and from this fact difficulties arise that are not met with in common commercial book-keeping. Having been so frequently consulted upon the subject of opening and closing the books of Joint Stock Companies by intelligent book-keepers, I am led to imagine a few practical suggestions upon the matter may be of much value.

To open the books for a simple partnership or a mercantile business, we only have to deal with positive values, whilst on opening the books for a compound partnership or a Joint Stock Company we are compelled to resort to values of another kind, namely, positive, nominal, and fictitious, and it is in the creation and disposition of these nominal and fictitious values that difficulties seem to arise.

The knowledge I have acquired upon the matter of compound partnerships has been from observation and study, coupled with a varied practical experience covering the better portion of my life, and I feel confident the various entries I shall here illustrate will assist the intelligent book-keeper, and go far to aid him in the disposition of all transactions to be encountered in the formation of a Joint Stock Company, no matter how complicated its organization may be.

I do not propose, even were I capable, to devote any of the pages of this little work to defining the law regulating Stock Concerns. That question I refer to some proper attorney, who should beyond question be consulted upon the first move looking toward any organization governed in the main by legal enactments. Nor shall I, like some authors, sacrifice golden hours, and exhaust the greater portion of my space in setting forth how articles of incorporation and other instruments of writing necessary to the formation of a Company should be executed. Neither shall its pages be encumbered with an exemplification of the minute book, or only a detail of the formula required to open the books for a Company that is to be blessed with a cash, paid-up capital.

My purpose here is not to theorize or to make book-keepers, but to deal, as it were, in "cold facts" with book-keepers already made. As it is to the intelligent who engage in the calling I appeal, I have no fears but that they will appreciate the many repetitions I purposely offer, as well as being capable of reasoning out the many seeming inconsistencies of my illustrations. Sad, indeed, must be the capacity of the book-keeper who is destitute of the ability to record the minutes of a "meeting," should that duty devolve upon him. While any first-class stationer can furnish books out of the ordinary run, such as Certificate Stock Book, Installment Book, Subscription Book, and the Stock Ledger, the forms and headings of which are all suggestive as to the disposition to be made of them. And the book-keeper who is lacking in genius to open a set of books for a Company which is to have a paid-up cash capital, certainly is not the person to be trusted to keep the accounts of a Joint Stock Concern.

All companies do not enjoy the advantage of having a paid-up cash capital. Some are obliged to operate upon a great deal less than their incorporated capital, while the capital of some may be conducted "all on paper," and sometimes "OTHERWISE." As a sample, two or more mercantile firms may consolidate. Upon these the foundation of a Joint Stock Concern is based, the members of which are to receive more or less Stock in return for the amount of net assets and other considerations they contribute. These two mercantile branches will say to the Company, "We donate you our assets; now take care of our liabilities." While each will say, "My interest in the old business was worth so much; give me Stock equal or in greater proportion to that interest."

Again, it frequently happens a large mercantile business incorporates into a Stock Company, the heads of which will donate a few shares to some few faithful employes, and divide the balance of Stock among themselves. These and many other transactions, too varied to mention, go to make up a class, whose affairs are not so simple to dispose of upon the books as they would be upon a cash basis. And it is to meet the many peculiarities that form these, I aim to contribute light, and I trust I shall succeed in assisting those who have only traveled in the straight rut of keeping accounts for a commercial business.

Trusting my readers may not accuse me of disparaging the merits of other works upon this subject, I remain,

Sincerely yours,

A. J. C.

CONTENTS.

....

CARNES' MANUAL

ON OPENING AND CLOSING

Books of Joint Stock Companies.

—◆•◆— — —

PROPOSITION I.

Organization of a Joint Stock Company.—Capital, $100,000.00.
1,000 Shares, par value, $100.—Manufacturing Steel Rails.
Incorporators agree to divide all the Stock among themselves, each to pay full par value per Share.

JOURNAL ENTRY.—EXAMPLE 1.

FRANCHISE, ... $100,000.00

For amount of the nominal value of the franchise of the Ohio Steel Rail Manufacturing
Company, together with all rights, titles,
and privileges, organized upon the basis of
$100,000.00 Capital Stock, divided into 1,000
shares of the nominal par value of $100
each, as per Articles of Incorporation,
dated December 26, 1883.

　　　　To CAPITAL STOCK, . . . $100,000.00

For amount of 1,000 shares of the par value
of $100, divided among and issued to the
incorporators and associates, as follows:

John Brown,	300 shares.	
W. Doe, . .	200	"
P. Smith,	100	"
H. Blake, .	350	"
A. J. Carnes. . .	50	"
	1,000	"

as per Stock Ledger.

Debit Franchise, and Credit Capital Stock Account, which two
accounts should remain open, one carried as an Asset, the other

as a Liability Account. Under the above agreement the Capital
Stock appears to be or will be paid up. That account, therefore,
should be left undisturbed. The Capital Stock Account must not be
affected unless by an act of the Board of Directors, the capital of the
Company be increased or decreased, which act, however, must be in
conformity with the law of the State in which the Company is located.

As the subscribers pay for their shares in *whole or in part*, issue
them their stock, and enter into the Cash Book, as follows:

EXAMPLE 2.

" To CONTINGENCIES,"

Received of John Brown, in full for his 300 *shares.* $30,000,00

As to the above Cash Book entry, the title of "Contingencies" is
used. This is a fictitious creation, and, therefore, has no value; but
may with propriety be used fictitiously, either as an asset or a liability, when necessary to get a real account upon the books. The experienced accountant, with little reasoning, will readily see an account
of this character can do no violation. It does not affect the gains or
losses; neither is it a liability to be paid. " *To installments*" would
answer, however, in the place of "Contingencies" when payments are
made in that way—in which case "Installments" would be credited
and carried (the same as "Contingencies") as a liability account.
(See Example 10.)

In this case open an account with "*Contingencies;*" credit that,
and debit cash. If the Company has been organized upon the fore-
going basis, the above entries will open the books. *After which, and
in all cases, proceed as in any ordinary book-keeping.*

Some accountants would in this case feel justified in opening an
account with each stockholder (see Stock Ledger). They would argue,
Mr. Blank is really a debtor to the Company as soon as he becomes a
subscriber. Whilst this is so, I fail to see how a claim for delinquency
on the part of Mr. Blank could any the more readily be substantiated
by having him charged upon the Ledger. The fact is, the subscription book shows Mr. Blank has subscribed for a certain number of
shares. That act lays him liable to lawful action should he refuse or
neglect to pay for the same.

Again, the incorporators of many corporations contribute a piece
of land, or a patent, or "something else," which forms the basis of

their Company; they, in consideration of this contribution, generally divide the voting shares among themselves, who never contemplate paying in one dollar, their aim being to make the Reserved Stock furnish money for operating purposes; in cases of this, and many similar kinds, it would not be a matter so easy to open an account with the Subscribers or Stockholders. But in this case, should the Company, after it has been operating, be compelled to tax the shareholders for an installment or an assessment, an entry in the Journal, "*Stockholders To Assessment*," would then be in order; but the matter of charging Stockholders and crediting Capital Stock is not so plain unless all the stock is sold for, or prospectively sold for, cash; but, as I have said, all companies have not that advantage. The following is the method alluded to:

JOURNAL ENTRY.—EXAMPLE 3.

STOCKHOLDERS. $100,000.00

To CAPITAL STOCK.   . $100,000.00

For amount of the Capital Stock of the Ohio Steel Rail Manufacturing Company, incorporated upon the basis of $100,000.00 Capital Stock, divided into 1,000 shares of the nominal par value of $100, issued to the incorporators and associates, as follows:

John Brown,	. 300	shares.
W. Doe,	200	"
P. Smith,	. 100	"
W. Blake, .	350	"
A. J. Carnes,	. 50	"
	1,000	"

as per Stock Ledger.

Debit Stockholders and credit Capital Stock. The above entry may be made upon the ground that the incorporators have agreed to take *all the stock* at its par value, and are therefore debtors; but suppose it was found in the course of operating that, after fifty per cent having been paid in, no more cash was needed, here you would have the account of Stockholders (or if an account had been opened with each Subscriber) owing a balance, the Company having declared no further installments or assessments would be necessary, it certainly would be wrong in effect and principle for an account having the appearance of a real Debtor to remain in that condition ; under such circumstances I should close the account " *Contingencies To Stockholders.*" If, after this operation, the Company should find itself obliged to make another " Call," open an account in the Journal " *Stockholders To Contingencies,*" this latter operation will open the Stockholders' account, to be closed when the assessment is paid.

Upon the same principle some accountants open the books by debiting Cash and crediting Capital Stock as installments are paid in, (See Stock Ledger.) If, as it appears to be in the case of the Ohio Steel Rail Manufacturing Company, 1,000 shares have been divided among the incorporators and others, this method would give Capital Stock account a credit of $25,000.00 on a call of twenty-five per cent, while $100,000.00, the nominal par value of 1,000 shares, would have been issued. The face value of 1,000 shares represent the incorporated Capital, therefore, should a call of twenty-five per cent be made, *and no more, or should the shares be sold above or below par, the Capital Stock Account is entitled to have credit for the full face value of* 1,000 *shares, i. e.* $100,000.00.

When a member of a body corporate who has subscribed for Stock with the understanding he was to pay its full par value, and then finds himself let off with fifty per cent, certainly claims and does receive dividends on the full face value of each share held by him, and he has the same claim if he buys Stock at a discount, and no greater claim if he buys Stock above par.

Or this entry :

JOURNAL ENTRY.—EXAMPLE 4.

CONTINGENCIES,   .   .   , $100,000.00
    (History.)

> To CAPITAL STOCK, $100,000.00
>   (History.)

If the Shareholders pay by installments or otherwise, debit Cash and credit " Contingencies ;" when all are paid in, the latter account will close. Should it be found that fifty per cent was sufficient, then carry what remains of Contingency as an Asset until closed by future installments, should any be called for. But as the incorporators and associates agreed to take all the stock at its par value, *the " Capital Stock " account must, upon the issue of the stock, receive credit for the full face value of shares issued. It is hardly sufficient to credit that account for only the per cent paid in, when the stock is issued.* (See Stock Ledger.) In the above case Contingency balance would be carried as an Asset, while the same account in the Cash Book (Example 2) would be carried as a Liability.

The following method may be preferred :

JOURNAL ENTRY.—EXAMPLE 5.

CERTIFICATES OF STOCK, $100,000.00

        TO CAPITAL STOCK, .   . $100,000.00

For amount of the Capital Stock of the Ohio Steel Rail Manufacturing Company, organized upon the basis of $100,000.00 Capital Stock, divided in 1,000 shares of the nominal par value of $100 each, appropriated to the incorporators and associates, as follows:

(Names of incorporators, see Example 3.)

As cash is received from the Subscribers debit Cash and credit Certificate of Stock account. Should the Company conclude that fifty per cent is sufficient, after having calculated on receiving the full value of the stock, I should, like in the preceding example, close Certificate of Stock account, "*By Contingencies.*" There would be no impropriety in carrying the balance of Certificate of Stock account, if that balance really represented stock unsold.

CLOSING THE BOOKS.

In all cases close into Profit and Loss the several accounts that belong there. Should that account show a gain or balance, say $5,000.00. close the account as follows :

JOURNAL ENTRY.—EXAMPLE 6.

PROFIT AND LOSS, .   . $5,000.00

        TO SURPLUS,   .   . $5,000.00

For amount of net gain, as appears by the Profit and Loss Account for the quarter ending March 31, 1884.

Open an account with surplus. Credit that and debit Profit and Loss, which operation will close that account. In preparing the Balance Sheet for the inspection of the Board of Directors, I think it best to close the Sheet "*To Net Gain*," as it may probably be better understood by those not skilled in accounts. But when you close your books use the title of Surplus. This account or its balance to be carried as a liability; but it must not operate for or against the gains of a subsequent quarter.

Some book-keepers prefer to carry the balance of " Profit and Loss," instead of " Surplus," as a proprietary Liability. They contend (and I think the point well taken) that " Profit and Loss" is easily understood. Many get it into their heads that " Surplus " represents actual Cash.

DIVIDENDS.

Now the gains appear to be $5,000.00. What per cent, if any, of that amount shall be paid in the shape of Dividends? In determining this question, there are several important points to be considered. First, what are the available Assets, *and what are the Liabilities that must be discharged? What contemplated improvements, machinery, etc., to be provided for, and how much Cash is there on hand?* It is true, the Net Gain is shown to be $5,000.00, yet there may be no Cash on hand. The balance of all expense accounts and losses having been closed into " Profit and Loss " account, it necessarily follows that the Cash, that should represent the Net Gain, has nearly all been expended in veritable assets. If by this reason there is no Cash on Hand, or if there is Cash on Hand and the interests of the Company need it in another direction, no well-managed Company would declare Dividends. Should, however, the Company see proper to depend upon early Maturities due them, they may with propriety borrow money to pay Dividends.

But it may happen, as in this instance, a large amount of money has been received from the sale of Stock. Consequently there is Cash on Hand for which there is no immediate use, whereupon the Board of Directors agree upon a twenty-five per cent Dividend on the Net Gain of $5,000,00.

JOURNAL ENTRY.—EXAMPLE 7.

SURPLUS,   . . $1,250.00

  To DIVIDEND No. 1, 1884, . . $1,250.00

For amount of twenty-five per cent Dividend
on $5,000.00 Net Gain, declared by order of
the Board of Directors, for the quarter ending March 31, 1884, at the sixth regular meeting April, 2, 1884.

Debit "Surplus" and credit "Dividend No. 1, 1884." As the
Stockholders receive their Dividends, take their receipt in a book
provided for that purpose. Credit "Cash" and debit "Dividend No.
1, 1884." When the Dividends have all been paid, foot the account.
Otherwise, if they have not all been paid, the account remains open
until all Dividends are paid.

Do not make one Dividend account a general reservoir for all the
Dividends. Open a new account for each quarter's Dividend declared.
Number them in regular order and the year, such as No. 2, 1884, No.
16, 1885, and so on. If a short corporation, group as many as convenient on one page, or reserve the space for short accounts in the back
of the Ledger. The accounts under this arrangement will prove convenient for those who have the right to inspect the books. Where
there are a great number of shareholders, your own judgment will
teach you what other provision should be made. *After a Dividend
has been declared, and the Stockholders so notified, it becomes a positive
Liability.*

STOCK LEDGER.

In ordering the Stock Ledger, have it constructed with a few
Ledger ruled pages in the fore part, upon one of which open an account with Capital Stock. Debit that with all the installments paid
and credit Stockholders' account with the same. This will leave the
Capital Stock account in a condition to show at any time how much
Cash has actually been paid in. All that is necessary after an incor-
porator or any person who has subscribed for Stock and paid a certain
sum thereon, is to issue them their Stock. Then open an account
with each in *this* Ledger. Credit them as follows: *Date and number
of certificate and the number of shares thereon (no value).* When Mr.
Brown pays, or if he has already paid any thing in the shape of an

installment, credit his account "*By Installment No.* 1, 10 *per cent,*
$300.00." Then debit Capital Stock account opened in the first part
of this Ledger for the same. This method will keep the Stock Ledger
in balance, and if it should be desired to learn who is and who is not
delinquent in their payments, a reference to·this Ledger will serve
you as well as if you had an account opened with each Stockholder
in the General Ledger, whilst the Subscription Book and the Capital
Stock account in the General Ledger will show how many shares have
been issued.

When a Stockholder actually transfers all or any portion of his
Stock, the original Certificate should be returned to the Company.
Paste the old Certificate to the stub from which it was first detached,
stamp the old Certificate across the face, "Cancelled March 31, 1884,"
note upon the stub to whom the transfer was made, and issue a new
Certificate for the shares so transferred. Should only part of the
shares named on the old Certificate be transferred, issue a new Certificate to the original owner for the number he retains, noting on the
old stub, "Renewed by No. 27," and on the stub of the new issue
note, "For No. 1, cancelled." Then debit his account in the Stock
Ledger as follows:

EXAMPLE 8.

Dr.									Cr.
DATE.	CERTIFICATES.	No. Shares.	Par Value.	DATE.	CERTIFICATES.	No. Shares.	Installments.	Par Value.
Mch. 16	Renewed by No. 27.	20		Jan. 1	No. 1...............	46		
" "	Transf. to J. Brown.	26						
				Mch. 16	No. 27..	20		

Now recredit his account for the new shares issued to him as
shown, then open an account with the party to whom the transfer was
made, and credit his account for the new shares issued to him. Postings into the Stock Ledger are made from the stub of the Certificate
of Stock book. *The buyer or seller of stock must, before the transfer is
made, pay for all unpaid installments or assessments.*

Certificates of Stock have printed on the reverse side a "Transfer
Form," but this does not prove convenient in cases where the party
desires to sell only a portion of the stock named upon the certificate,

and sometimes fractions of stock are both sold and transferred from the original.   Neither is it absolutely essential to use a transfer book, entries made on the stub of the Certificate Stock book by the proper officer, as I have shown, being all that is necessary.

But should you open the books by debiting Stockholders and crediting Capital Stock Account for installments due, or debit Cash for installments paid and credit Capital Stock Account for the same from the Cash book direct to the main Ledger, then you must change the order of the Capital Stock Account in the Stock Ledger, that is to say, charge that account with the par value of the shares issued, and credit each Shareholder for the same.   The Stock Ledger will then show the amount of stock issued. while the Capital Stock Account in the main Ledger will show how much has been paid in, but this, I contend, is improper, the amount of stock issued is a part of the business of the Company, hence. its face value should be credited in the main Ledger ; and I prefer using fictitious accounts when necessary for that purpose.

PROPOSITION II.

Organization of a Joint Stock Company.—Capital $100,000.00. 1,000 Shares, Par Value $100.—Majority of Stock Divided among the Incorporators, they to pay $10 per Share, Balance of Stock Reserved for Working or Operating Capital. Company Contract to Pay for Machinery or Real Estate, Part in Cash and Part in Stock.—Money Borrowed to Pay Dividends.—Dividends Declared and Paid in Stock.

JOURNAL ENTRY.—EXAMPLE 9.

FRANCHISE   TO SUNDRIES,   - $100,000.00

> For amount of the nominal value of the Franchise of the Star Rolling Mills Company, with all rights, titles, claims, and privileges, organized upon the basis of $100,000.00 Capital Stock, divided into 1,000 shares of the nominal par value of $100 each.

To CAPITAL STOCK,   .   ,   .   . $60,000.00

> For amount of six hundred Shares of the par value of $100, divided among the Incorporators and Associates at $10 per share (subject to additional assessment), as follows:

A. J. Carnes. . . .	300 shares.
W. Small, . . .	100 "
J. Adams, . . .	50 "
James Otis, . . .	50 "
Silas Wright, . .	100 "
	600 "

> as per Stock Ledger.

To WORKING CAPITAL,   .   .   . $40,000.00

> For amount of four hundred Shares of the Capital Stock, reserved to be sold, the proceeds to be applied for operating purposes.

Debit Franchise, credit Capital Stock, and credit Working Capital. The incorporators have, in the above case, received $60,-000.00 worth of stock, even though they should never be called upon to pay any thing additional to the $10 per share. The Capital Stock, nevertheless, is nominally paid up to the extent of $60,000,00. (Now call the agreed ten per cent.)

JOURNAL ENTRY.—EXAMPLE 10.

SUNDRIES TO INSTALLMENT NO. 1 (*or Assessment No. 1*). $6,000.

A. J. Carnes, his 10% on 300 shares,	$3,000,00
W. Small, his 10% on 100 shares,	1,000.00
J. Adams, his 10% on 50 shares,	500.00
James Otis, his 10% on 50 shares,	500.00
Silas Wright, his 10% on 100 shares,	1,000.00

For amount of first installment of ten per cent called on 600 Shares of the Capital Stock, issued to the above incorporators and associates, as per agreement.

When they pay their ten per cent, credit off their accounts, then issue them their stock. (*See Stock Ledger*). Carry Installment No. 1 as a liability account, and number the installments or assessments in regular order. Now suppose, as is done by some book-keepers, the books were opened as shown by the latter example—Stockholders individually debited, and *"Capital Stock" credited*, after which no more installments should be required—they, the Stockholders, would be holding stock representing $60,000.00 while the Capital Stock account would only be credited with $6,000.00, the amount paid in. *When Shares are delivered upon payment of the first installment, the Capital Stock is nominally paid up to the nominal par value of the Certificates of Stock issued.*

RESERVE SHARES SOLD AT PAR.

JOURNAL ENTRY.—EXAMPLE 11.

CERTIFICATES OF STOCK, . .	$1,000,00	
To CAPITAL STOCK, . .		$1,000.00

For amount of ten shares of Reserved Shares sold at par.

When the cash is received, debit that, and credit off Certificate of Stock Account. This operation need not affect the Working Capital Account. Still carry, or what remains of, that account as a liability: or an entry, "*Working Capital*" *To* "*Capital Stock*," *could have been made.* When the cash is paid, credit Working Capital Account. Or again, in this case, as the full par value of the ten shares have been paid for in cash, Cash could be debited and Capital Stock credited without regard to the Journal, but I maintain all transactions affecting the stock should have their history upon the Journal, as I have shown.

RESERVED SHARES SOLD BELOW PAR.

JOURNAL ENTRY.—EXAMPLE 12.

SUNDRIES	To CAPITAL STOCK,	$1,000,00

For amount of ten shares of the Reserved
Shares, sold at fifty dollars per share.

A. J. CARNES,   .   .   . $500.00

For amount of ten shares of the Capital Stock
issued to him at fifty per cent discount by
order, etc., etc.

WORKING CAPITAL,   .   .   . $500.00

. For amount of fifty per cent discount on ten
shares.

Here you will notice stock has been sold at a discount, but Capital Stock has received credit for the full face value of the ten shares, all the same. Close his account from the Cash book.

RESERVED STOCK SOLD AT A PREMIUM.

JOURNAL ENTRY.—EXAMPLE 13.

A. J. CARNES   To SUNDRIES, $1,100.00

For amount of ten shares of the Reserved
Stock sold to him at $1.10 per share.

To CAPITAL STOCK, $1,000.00

Par value of ten shares.

To WORKING CAPITAL,   . $100.00

For amount of ten per cent premium received
on ten shares of Reserved Shares.

In the last two transactions the Reserved Stock has been sold both above and below par, an apparent gain and loss. *Whilst this is so, it is not that class of loss or gain that should affect the legitimate gains of the business.*

JOURNAL ENTRY.—EXAMPLE 14.

REAL ESTATE,　　To SUNDRIES,　.　$10,000.00

For amount of the value of Warehouse, No. 36 East Third Street, Cincinnati, Ohio, purchased of John Ing, Jr., for $10,000.00, transferred to the Company by him by Deed dated July 26, 1884, recorded among the Land Records of Hamilton County, State of Ohio, Liber 226, Folio 236, to be paid for part in Cash and part in Stock

　　　To JOHN ING, JR.,　.　.　$5,000.00

For balance due him for and on account of purchase of Warehouse, No. 36 East Third Street, Cincinnati, Ohio.

　　　To CAPITAL STOCK, .　.　.　5,000.00

For amount of 50 shares of the par value of $100, of the Reserved Stock, transferred to John Ing, Jr., in part payment of Warehouse, No. 36 East Third Street, Cincinnati, Ohio, as per Stock Ledger.

If a Mortgage be given in part, it must take the place of John Ing, Jr., in the above, when the Cash is paid his account will close.

MONEY BORROWED TO PAY DIVIDENDS.

First close the net gain or loss into surplus.

JOURNAL ENTRY.—EXAMPLE 15.

CASH (*Posted from C. B.*),　　　$5,000.00

　　　To BILLS PAYABLE (*or Mortgage*)　　$5,000.00

For amount of $5,000.00, on our note dated April 2, 1884, 60 days, favor of and discounted at the Third National Bank, Cincinnati, Ohio, to pay the third quarter's dividend, ending March 31, 1884, by order of Board of Directors, at the 12th regular meeting, April 1, 1884.

Now the following entry:

SURPLUS,　.　.　.　.　.　.　$5,000.00　　.

　　　To DIVIDEND No. 3, 1884,　　.　$5,000.00
　　　　　　　(History.)

When the dividends are paid, that account will close. The Cash received from the note could have been carried to the Cash Book direct, and the Journal avoided entirely. *But borrowing money for such purposes is an important transaction : its history should be given in full upon the Journal.*

TO PAY STOCK DIVIDENDS, &c.

Should stock be sold or issued to pay dividends after the original incorporated Capital has been disposed of, the Company could be justly held for " *watering*." There must be a lawful increase of stock.

FIFTY PER CENT DIVIDEND DECLARED ON $5,000.00.

JOURNAL ENTRY.—EXAMPLE 16.

PROFIT AND LOSS,   To SUNDRIES, $5,000.00

For amount of $5,000.00 net gain, as appears
by the Profit and Loss Account for the
quarter ending March 31, 1884.

    To CAPITAL STOCK, $2,500.00

For amount of fifty per cent dividend declared
on $5,000.00 net gain, in payment of which
25 shares of the reserved Stock of the
par value of $100 has been issued to the
Stockholders, by order of the Board of
Directors, at the tenth regular meeting,
April 2, 1884.

    To SURPLUS, .   .   . $2,500.00

For amount of $2,500.00, the balance of
$5,000.00, net gain for the quarter ending
March 31, 1884.

Had the Profit and Loss Account shown a very small gain or loss, these balances should be closed into " Surplus," then another form of entry would be required.

JOURNAL ENTRY.—EXAMPLE 17.

WORKING CAPITAL,   .   . $2,500.00

    To CAPITAL STOCK,   . $2,500.00

For amount of 25 shares of the nominal par
value of $100, of the Reserved Shares, issued
•in payment of a Stock Dividend declared
by the Board of Directors, at their tenth
regular meeting, April 2, 1884.

AGAIN.

$2,500.00 Dividend declared and paid for with Reserved Stock, the shares delivered to the Stockholders at fifty per cent discount.

JOURNAL ENTRY.—EXAMPLE 18.

WORKING CAPITAL. . . . $5,000.00

To CAPITAL STOCK, . . $5,000.00

For amount of $2,500.00 Stock Dividend, in
payment of which 50 shares of the nominal
par value of $100 of the Reserved Stock has
been issued to and divided among the Stockholders at 50 per cent discount, by order of
the Board of Directors, at their tenth regular
meeting, April 2, 1884.

Or to pay a Stock Dividend, make this entry :

JOURNAL ENTRY.—EXAMPLE 19.

WORKING CAPITAL. . . . $2,500,00

To DIVIDEND No. 2, 1884, . . $2,500.00
    (History.)

Then,

DIVIDEND No. 2, 1884. $2,500.00

To CAPITAL STOCK, . . . $2,500.00
    (History.)

PROPOSITION III

A Commercial Business Incorporated into a Joint Stock Company upon the Basis of $400,000.00 Capital Stock, 8,000
Shares, Par Value, $50.

The above commercial business was composed of three partners,
whose combined capital, as shown by the books, was $200,000.00, of
which J. Blake's share was $100,000.00, S. Blake's share was $50,-
000.00, and H. Blake's share was also $50,000.00. In order to in-
corporate, two gentlemen, D and E, are induced to join them, they
each to subscribe for 1,000 shares of the stock, and to pay ten per
cent down, the balance to be paid by installments. The three origi-

nal partners agree to divide the remaining 6,000 shares among themselves in proportion to their net capital in the old business.

The Assets and Liabilities of the old firm are, (Partners and worthless accounts thrown out):

Merchandise,	. .	$100,000.00	Bills Payable, . .	$50,000.00
Personal Accounts		55,000.00	Personal Accounts,	50,000,00
Bills Receivable,	.	25,000.00	J. Blake's Share, .	100,000.00
Machinery	.	60,000.00	S. Blake's "	50,000.00
Real Estate,	.	60,000.00	H. Blake's " .	50,000.00
		$300,000.00		$300,000.00

From the above it will be seen the Assets are $300,000.00, and the Liabilities are $100,000.00, forming the basis upon which a Capital Stock of $400,000.00 is to be created. Under the agreed division, J. B. will have 3,000 shares, S. B. will have 1,500 shares, H. B. 1,500 shares, while D and E will have 1,000 shares each.

JOURNAL ENTRY.—EXAMPLE 20.

SUNDRIES   TO CAPITAL STOCK,   .   . $400,000.00

FRANCHISE, ... $300,000.00

For amount of the nominal value of the Franchise of the Blake Paper Manufacturing Company, with all rights, titles, and privileges, organized upon the basis of $400,000.00 Capital Stock divided into 8,000 shares of the par value of $50, of which 6,000 shares are appropriated as follows:

J. Blake,	.	3,000	shares.
S. Blake,	.	1,500	"
H. Blake,	. .	1,500	"

as per Stock Ledger.

CERTIFICATES OF STOCK,   . $100,000.00

For amount of 2,000 shares, of the par value of $50, of the Capital Stock of the Blake Paper Manufacturing Company (being the remaining shares of the original 8,000 shares), issued as follows:

D,		1,000	shares.
E.	.	. 1,000	"

| SUNDRIES | To CONTINGENCIES, | . | $300,000.00 |

Merchandise,	. .	$100,000.00
Personal Accounts,	.	55,000.00
Bills Receivable,		25.000.00
Machinery,	.	60,000.00
Real Estate,		60,000.00

For amount of all approved property, duly
inventoried and recorded in Stock Book
July 6, 1884, transferred to the Company by
J. Blake, S. Blake, and H. Blake, for which
they have accepted 6,000 shares of the Capital Stock of the Blake Paper Manufacturing Company, divided among themselves as
per agreement dated July 6, 1884, recorded
in this Journal, page 21. (The agreement
entire may follow this entry).

CONTINGENCIES	To SUNDRIES	$100,000.00
	To BILLS PAYABLE,	.	,	.	$50,000.00
	To PERSONAL ACCOUNTS,	. .	$50,000.00

For amount of all approved Liabilities, duly
inventoried and recorded in Stock Book
July 6, 1884, the same being owing by J.
Blake, S. Blake, and H. Blake, and by them
transferred to the Company, of which the
Company has assumed the payment, by an
agreement dated July 6, 1884, and recorded
in this Journal, page 26.

Debit " Franchise," debit " Certificates of Stocks," credit "Capital
Stock," debit each one of the several Assets, and credit " Contingen-
cies " " By Sundries; " then credit each of the several " Liabilities,"
and debit " Contingencies " " To Sundries." (Certificate of Stock
Account may be at once closed by *"Installment To Certificate of Stock."*)
As D and E pay the agreed installments credit Certificates of Stock
Account, and debit Cash. Some accountants would open an account
with Blake Paper Manufacturing Company in place of " Franchise."
Of course you don't lump each account as here shown.

Here is another form of entry :

JOURNAL ENTRY.—EXAMPLE 21.

FRANCHISE   TO SUNDRIES, $400,000.00
                      (History.)

                   TO CAPITAL STOCK. $300,000.00
                      (History.)

                   TO WORKING CAPITAL.* $100,000.00
                      (History.)

ASSETS
          TO CONTINGENCIES.

CONTINGENCIES

          TO LIABILITIES.

Carry Working Capital Account, or what remains of it, as a Liability. When D and E are called upon for their installments, enter

INSTALLMENT No. 1
          TO CAPITAL STOCK.
             (History.)
     Or
D AND E (*First Installment*)†
          TO CAPITAL STOCK.
             (History.)
Or open with the following entries :

JOURNAL ENTRY.—EXAMPLE 22.

SUNDRIES		TO	SUNDRIES.	
Franchise, . . .	$100,000.00	Capital Stock, .	400,000.00	
Assets, . .	300,000.00	Liabilities. .	100,000.00	
D,†	50,000.00			
E,†	$ 50,000,00			

See Proposition VIII, Consolidations.

*See Proposition II, Example 9.
†In this case, as installments are called, Capital Stock can be credited. This entry may be justified upon the ground that D and E will pay, and when paid their accounts will close.

Should a mercantile firm, about to incorporate into a Joint Stock Company, comprise enough members to incorporate under the law, and agree to divide ALL the stock among themselves according to their interest in the old firm, first find the sum of the total Liabilities, to which add the total sum of the incorporated Capital, from the total sum of all these you will deduct the total sum of the new appraised Assets, the amount remaining you must charge to "Franchise," or some book-keepers might use the name of the Company instead of "Franchise" (I think, however, the latter the best title). Now issue the stock to the partners as understood; then credit all in the Stock Ledger for the Number and Face Value of their certificates, and debit Capital Stock account in the same Ledger for the same.

Street Railways.

Books of Street Railways, in relation to the stock account, can be made up from illustrations shown herein, as the author takes for granted book-keepers know all the elements that go to Profit and Loss therefore make no suggestion on that point, any more than to say in the matter of the Horse and Mule Account, some roads scale the loss of that property from 60 to as low as 20 per cent. The manner of Cash returns between Conductor and Receiver, of course, is not a matter of book-keeping, but a subject left to the ingenuity on part of those in authority; in this respect the system inaugurated in the Receiver's department of the Baltimore City Passenger Railway Company is the best the author has seen, and perhaps the best in the country.

PROPOSITION IV.

A commercial business with $20,000.00 in Assets and no Liabilities, incorporate into a Joint Stock Company.—Capital, $50,000.00.—Majority of Stock divided among the incorporators.

JOURNAL ENTRY.—EXAMPLE 23.

SUNDRIES   To   SUNDRIES.

Franchise,   , $30,000.00
(History.)

Assets,   20,000,00
(History.)

To CAPITAL STOCK,   .   .   . $40,000.00
(Divided among the incorporators.)

To WORKING CAPITAL,   .   10,000.00
(History.)

Now the same business has $20,000.00 in speculative Assets and a *Steam Engine that cost* $10,000.00 incorporated as above.

JOURNAL ENTRY.—EXAMPLE 24.

SUNDRIES   To   SUNDRIES.

Machinery,   . $30,000.00
(Nominal value.)

Assets,   20,000.00
(History.)

To CAPITAL STOCK,   . $40,000,00
(History.)

To WORKING CAPITAL,   10,000.00
(History.)

The actual cost of the Engine was $10,000.00; but it is entered up at the nominal value of $30,000.00. To this there is no objection, as it is not a speculative resource. Or charge the Engine at $10,-000.00, and give the balance, $20,000,00 to Franchise.

PROPOSITION V.

A gentleman with no money has a Patent Rake.—He finds several capitalists, who incorporate a Joint Stock Company for the purpose of manufacturing the Rake.—They agree to pay the patentee " Smith" $5,000.00 in Stock for his patent.—Capital Stock, $100,000.00.—1,000 shares, $100 par value.—Each of the incorporators subscribe for as many shares as they wish.

JOURNAL ENTRY.—EXAMPLE 25.

SMITH PATENT, . . .	$5,000.00	
To CAPITAL STOCK, . .		$5,000,00

For amount of 50 shares of Stock of the nominal par value of $100 of the Capital Stock of the Cincinnati Patent Rake Manufacturing Company, incorporated upon the basis of $100,000.00 Capital, said 50 shares issued to John Smith in payment for all his right, title, claim, and interest in and to his Patent Rake, transferred to the Company by him, by Deed dated March 2, 1884, recorded in this Journal, page 26. (Embrace a copy of the Deed in this entry.)

FRANCHISE To SUNDRIES,	$95,000.00	
(History.)		
To CAPITAL STOCK, .		$55,000.00

For amount of 550 shares of the nominal par value of $100 of the Capital Stock of the Cincinnati Patent Rake Manufacturing Company, divided among the incorporators as follows:

A,	200 shares.
B, .	300 "
C, . .	30 "
D, . . , .	20 "

As per Stock Ledger.

To WORKING CAPITAL,	.	$40,000.00

See Prop. II, Ex. 8. (History.)

Debit Smith's Patent, credit Capital Stock, debit Franchise, credit Capital Stock, and credit Working Capital.

The Capital Stock is nominally paid up to the extent of $5,000.00 in one case and $55,000.00 in the other ; after which, when a call is made upon the incorporators for money, *debit them collectively or individually, and credit Installment or Assessment No. 1.* If any of the Reserved Shares are sold to new buyers, debit Working Capital and credit "Capital Stock." (See other Prop.)

The following will open the books for the same case :

JOURNAL ENTRY.—EXAMPLE 26.

SMITH'S PATENT   To   SUNDRIES, $100,000.00

For the amount of the nominal value of John Smith's Patent Rake, transferred to the Cincinnati Patent Rake Manufacturing Company, by him, by Deed of Assignment, dated March 2, 1884, recorded in this Journal, page 2. (Copy Deed in this entry.)

To CAPITAL STOCK,   . $5,000.00

For amount of 50 shares of the nominal par value of $100 of the Capital Stock of the Cincinnati Patent Rake Manufacturing Company, organized upon the basis of $100,000 Capital Stock, divided into 1,000 shares. Said 50 shares have been issued to John Smith for his Patent Rake, deeded to the Company by him with all rights, titles, and claims to him belonging.

To CAPITAL STOCK,   . $55,000.00

For amount of 550 shares of the nominal par value of $100 of the Capital Stock of the Cincinnati Patent Rake Manufacturing Company, divided among the incorporators as follows :

A,   .   200 shares,
B,   .   .   300   "
C,   30   "
D,   .   .   20   "

As per Stock Ledger.

To WORKING CAPITAL, $40,000.00

See Prop. II, Ex. 9. (History.)

In the two preceding series of entries, "Smith's Patent" is charged in one case $5,000,00, the apparent cost, while in the other it is charged $100,000.00. This latter rate is only a nominal value given, and can have no effect. The Company can, without violation, rate its value as it chooses. It must not be understood by this that a company can place nominal values on the Speculative Resources, Expense Accounts, or Positive Liabilities; but in opening the books a nominal value may be given to such properties as "Mine," "Machinery," "Land," "Steamboat," "Franchise," either to increase or decrease, without being at fault.

PROPOSITION VI.

An owner of a piece of land meets with a party of gentlemen, who agree to pay him $10,000 to donate the land for the purpose of incorporating a Joint Stock Company.—The land is supposed to contain minerals, and it is for the purpose of developing this supposed product the Company is formed. The incorporators (of which body it is agreed the owner is to be one) are to divide the controlling shares among themselves, the balance of shares to be sold for operating purposes.—Capital, $100,000.00, 1,000 shares, $100 each.

JOURNAL ENTRY.—EXAMPLE 27.

LAND ACCOUNT   To   SUNDRIES.   . $100,000.00

For the appraised value of 600 acres of land, located in Hamilton County, State of Ohio, donated to the Miami Iron and Steel Manufacturing Company by A. J. Carnes, together with all his rights, titles, claims, and privileges, as per Deed dated March 22, 1883, said Company incorporated upon the basis of $100,000.00 Capital Stock, divided into 1,000 shares of the nominal par value of $100 each.

        To CAPITAL STOCK. $60,000.00
    (Amount divided among incorporators, etc.)

        To WORKING CAPITAL, $40,000.00
                (History.)

The title of "Land Account" could be changed to "Mine Account," "Franchise Account," "Real Estate Account," or "Plant Account," followed by the same history already applied to Land Account. For treatment of Working Capital Account see other Propositions.

PROPOSITION VII.

Now upon another plan.—We will suppose the $10,000 paid is not to go to the owners' own individual use, but is to be applied to operate the Company, for which he, the owner, is to be one of the incorporators and is also to receive the majority of Stock (501 shares), and the other associates to receive a certain agreed number of shares, to be divided among themselves.

JOURNAL ENTRY.—EXAMPLE 28.

SUNDRIES   To   SUNDRIES.

Franchise,   .   . $90,000.00

For the nominal value of the Franchise, etc.

Investment,   .   .   .   10,000.00

For the amount of $10,000.00 contributed to the Company by the incorporators and associates, etc.

   To CAPITAL STOCK, $60,000.00

Shares divided among the incorporators, etc.

   To WORKING CAPITAL, $40,000.00
     (History.)

Now carry the $10,000.00 to the Cash Book, and enter "*To Investment.*" When that is posted, "Investment Account" will be closed. The preceding Propositions will furnish the history to entries where none are given. "Contingencies" may be substituted for "Investment."

PROPOSITION VIII.

CONSOLIDATIONS.

Consolidation of the B. B. & C. L. and the Tuscaloosa Narrow Gauge Railways.

Condition of affairs have compelled these two Roads to consolidate. Both are burdened with a large floating debt, upon which interest is due and unpaid. The Stock of both is " way down," so to speak, and is worth nothing. In round numbers, $4,000,000.00 worth of the Stock of each of these Companies is held by clamorous holders.

The proposed Company to be incorporated out of the above two Companies agree not to repudiate this old Stock, but to receive it at its par value in exchange for new Stock. The floating debt of each of the old corporations, as well as all interest due thereon, is to be assumed by the new Company. The Capital Stock of the latter is to be $12,000,000.00, divided into 120,000 shares of the nominal par value of $100, of which 80,000 shares will be required to take up the old Stock, leaving 40,000 shares to be sold for operating purposes, and the new Company also agree to issue $1.000,000.00 worth of six per cent bonds.

First make up a sum of the Assets and Liabilities of one of the old Companies, including the old Stock to be redeemed at its face value, as follows :

JOURNAL ENTRY.—EXAMPLE 29.

ASSETS.

Construction and Equipment.	$3.000,000.00
Bonds U. S. 6s.,	60,000.00
Interest due on U. S. Bonds.	1,800.00
B. B. & C. L. (old Stock),	4,000,000.00
Due from other Roads,	25,000.00
	$7,086,800.00

LIABILITIES.

1st Mortgage Bonds, 1860, outstanding,	$600,000.00
2d " " 1870, "	600,000.00
Interest due on 1st Mortgage Bonds, 1860,	15,000.00
" " " 2d " " 1870,	30,000.00
Bills Payable,	30,000.00
Due to other Roads.	25,000.00
Other Indebtedness,	30,000.00
	$1,330,000.00

In the same manner detail and sum up the Assets (adding the face value of the old Stock to be redeemed) and the Liabilities of the other Company. Give each Company's property a separate Journal Entry, with a full and complete history and description of each

item of property; (same rule for mercantile firms.) *Then take the total
sum of the Liabilities of the two Companies, add to that the Capital
Account to the extent of $8,000,000.00 new Stock (to be issued in exchange
for the Stock of the old Companies), and the amount of $4,000,000.00
reserved, to be sold for operating.' From the total of all these you will
deduct the total Assets, including the amount of old Stock of the two
Companies. The balance thus remaining charge to "Franchise."* After
this operation you will have equal "Assets" and "Liabilities," and
the work will be ready for the Journal thus:

JOURNAL ENTRY.—EXAMPLE 30.

SUNDRIES	To	SUNDRIES	
1st Co's Assets, . . .	$3,086,800.00	Capital Stock, (*Exchange*	
1st Co's Old Stock, .	4,000,000.00	*for Old Stock*), .	$8,000,000.00
2d Co's Assets, .	3,000,000.00	Working Capital, .	4,000,000.00
2d Co's Old Stock, .	4,000,000.00	1st Co's Liabilities, .	1,330,000.00
Franchise (*Balance*), .	1,243,200.00	2d Co's Liabilities, . .	2,000,000.00
	$15,330,000.00		$15,330,000.00

Do not neglect to add the full history to each of the above properties. Should the worthless stock be redeemed at five per cent, then
debit each with $200,000.00, and credit Capital Stock Account with
$400,000.00, after which apply the balance of new stock to Working
Capital Account. It is more than probable the Liabilities of two
such companies would exceed their Assets, in which event there would
be a greater amount to be charged to Franchise; or, instead of creat-
ing the Account of Franchise, take the balance that go to make that
account and divide it up, and increase the many different properties
that go to make up the "Construction and Equipment" Account; or
one account may be increased, that is to say, add one-half of this
balance to the value of the track of one Company, the other half to
the track of the other Company; this operation will give the tracks a
nominal value.

In the above operation the worthless stock, to which a nominal
value is given, is taken to account as an Asset. To this there can be
no objection. It is true the stock is worthless, yet a value has been
given for it; hence to carry it as an Asset can do no violation. It
neither disturbs the operations of the Company nor affects the gains
or losses; besides, the Company may require it upon the books for
future reference. This worthless stock could be discarded from the

books entirely, in which case the amount that goes to make up that account could be added to " Franchise," or to the value of some fixed property comprising " Equipment and Construction " should the worthless stock not be taken to account: then the amount of $8,000,000.00, credited to Capital Stock, must be followed by a history for what and to whom the stock was issued. The opening entries here can be applied to opening the books for the consolidation of two or more mercantile firms.

The bonds to be issued *are not a liability until actually sold or otherwise disposed of,* although I have seen book-keepers, when bonds were placed in the hands of brokers or agents to sell, charge them and credit Bonds Payable in the General Ledger. This is wrong, because bonds are not a liability while in the hands of a broker or agent, nor can either of these be treated as debtors while acting for the Company. Should they, however, report sales and hold the proceeds, it may then be proper to charge them, because the Company becomes responsible for its bonds when legitimately sold. As the bonds are sold from time to time for cash or otherwise disposed of, debit that and credit Bonds Payable.

PROPOSITION IX.

In some companies it may happen after the incorporators and associates have divided up the entire stock among themselves, may, for certain reasons, conclude to donate a portion of their shares, to the amount of say $40,000.00, to the company for the purpose of raising more funds In this case *debit Capital Stock, and open an account with Working Capital, and credit that. Should any of the donated shares be sold, debit Cash, and credit Capital Stock Account: If these shares are to be sold at a discount,* make the following entry :

JOURNAL ENTRY.—EXAMPLE 31.

WORKING CAPITAL.

To CAPITAL STOCK.

(History.)

The only further entries required would be to debit each Shareholder's account in the Stock Ledger for the number of shares donated,

such as " *Transferred To the Company* 20 *shares.*"   Of course the original certificates will have to be returned to the Company, and can-
celed, and new shares issued.   This is particularly the case where the
original certificates call for all the shares held by any one shareholder.

Reserved Fund

Is a fund set aside for some or any special purpose, and should always
represent actual Cash.   The Cash should be taken from the Common
Cash, and have a separate Bank Account, with extra Check and Bank
Book.

Journal Entry.

Reserved Fund (See Ex. 15),   .   .   .$20,000.00

       To Cash (*posted from C. B.*)   . $20,000.00
       (History.)

    This operation takes $20,000.00 from the Common Cash, and
places it into the Reserved Fund.

    To purchase Real Estate or any thing out of the Reserved Fund,
first take $10,000.00 out of the Reserved Fund, and replace it into
the Common Cash as follows :

Cash (*posted from C. B.*),   . $10,000.00

       To Reserved Fund, $10,000.00
       (History.)

    To buy the property :

Real Estate,   .   . $10,000.00

       To John Clark,   . $10,000.00
       (History.)

To pay dividends out of the Reserved Fund :

SURPLUS,

To DIVIDEND No. 2, 1884.

(History.)

Then,

CASH (*posted from C. B.*)

To RESERVED FUND.

(History.)

Then,

DIVIDEND No. 2, 1884,

To CASH (*posted from C. B.*)

(History.)

The above Cash Entries might be omitted from the Journal entirely ; but I do not think it advisable to do so, especially when connected with important transactions. "Short Cuts" may answer in the books of a simple mercantile business ; but in a Joint Stock Concern numerous advantages are gained in giving complete details to transactions likely to be inquired into at any time. The Reserved Fund could have been credited direct ; but I think it best to bring the Cash back into the Common Cash, as I have shown.

A. J. Carnes has to his credit the amount of $4.861.72, and agrees to take $10,000.00 worth of Stock for his claim.

JOURNAL ENTRY.—EXAMPLE 32.

SUNDRIES   To   CAPITAL STOCK,   . $10,000.00

A. J. CARNES,   .   . $4,861.72

For amount of 100 shares transferred to him
in payment, etc.

WORKING CAPITAL, ... $5,138.28

Discount on 100 shares transferred to A. J.
Carnes, etc,

BALANCE SHEET. No. 1.

Draw off all the balances from the General Ledger. Find the gross gains in the usual way. *Before closing the Sheet, and apart from the Ledger, ascertain how much rent, wages, taxes, and interest not charged is due and unpaid up to that time. These amounts you will add to the debit side of the Profit and Loss Account, and credit the same under the head of Liabilities. Then find how much rent, interest, etc., not charged is due the Company and unpaid up to that time (these you will add to the debit of Assets), and credit the Profit and Loss Account with the same.* Now close the Sheet, and you will be nearer the true gains, upon which it would be safer to declare Dividends. Besides this, you would have a proper statement of affairs.

BALANCE SHEET, No. 2.

But as you may not desire, neither may it be practicable, to close the books from the above, draw off the balances in the ordinary way from the Ledger, without reference to the several items not charged, and close the books.

Present No. 1 to *each one of the Board*, with No. 2 attached. The reason for this is, should you offer only No. 1 when you have closed your books from No. 2, you might find yourself going through the ordeal of trying to explain to some one of the Directors, why it is the balance account on the Ledger does not agree with the Balance Sheet you gave him at the last "meetin'."

‹♦—✳·‹♦

MISCELLANEOUS.

Read all the preceding propositions attentively: the intelligent book-keeper will find sufficient material to suit his case.

A subscriber neglecting or refusing to pay a lawful installment is not only liable to the law, but is chargeable with interest on the same.

A stockholder is not entitled to a vote if any of the calls upon the shares held by him are in arrears.

To furnish ready information, each quarterly interest should have an account to itself in the Ledger in regular order, such as "*Coupon Interest, March* 31, 1884." Do not make a general reservoir of one account, as I have seen some book-keepers do; neither charge one quarter's interest for money paid on another quarter's interest.

When coupons or script are paid, cancel them and paste in a book prepared for that purpose. By this operation you will have it easy of access in case an examination is required.

In a Stock Company (limited) the shareholders each are liable to the creditors to the extent of their shares. To omit the word "Limited" in a company of this character is unlawful for every omission.

A company without the word "Limited" affixed is understood to be a full Liability. In a full Liability Company a Stockholder individually is liable for the full indebtedness of the company. Suit, however, in all cases must first be brought against the company.

Bonds are not a Liability until sold or disposed of, and not until then do they have an account in the Ledger.

When a company has organized and complied with the terms of the law, the law is indifferent as to the amount of money afterwards paid in. Neither does the law care whether you sell your stock for five or fifty cents on the dollar, but it may interest itself as to the amount of stock that is being issued; hence the Capital Stock Account, as I have shown, should receive credit for the nominal value of each share sold or otherwise disposed of. That account is supposed to show to what amount the stock has been issued, and not, as imagined by some book-keepers, the amount paid in. My method of manipulating the Stock Ledger will furnish that information.*

In some short corporations, when the members are and continue to be harmonious, a great many acts are committed that would not be sanctioned by law. But in long corporations, or where there are a great many members, a strict regard for all details should be closely observed.

The laws of all States require a certain per cent. to be paid in on the part of the incorporators and associates before articles of incorporation can be filed. On the other hand, some companies are formed and go on and continue to operate without regard to law.

After the books are opened, should there be no more stock on hand, or if there is stock on hand and the accounts of " Working Capital," " Contingencies," " Assessments " or " Installments," should not be closed, carry each as a proprietary asset or liability.

In opening the books first find how much stock is divided among the incorporators, the amount of which must be credited to " Capital Stock," the balance you will credit to " Working Capital," this operation gets all the sold and unsold stock upon the Ledger. " Working Capital " may also receive credit for amount prospectively sold for the purpose of running certain transactions through the books. (See Proposition III, Example 21.)

After you have opened the books for a consolidation, or for a simple partnership incorporated into a Joint Stock Company, should it be discovered an Asset or a Liability has been omitted, or any thing received for which no apparent value has been given, use " Contingencies " as a balancing medium (some book-keepers use the name of the company) to get the omitted transaction upon the books. The same account may be used should it happen that the company become possessed of money in the way of damages, gift, etc. This latter property, however, although not strictly an operating gain, may, by mutual consent, be credited to Profit and Loss Account for the purpose of dividing it up into dividends. Should the money be designed for the Reserved Fund, use "Contingencies;" credit that and debit Cash, then from Cash to the "Reserved Fund."

All agreements, contracts, and every thing necessary to the formation of a Joint Stock Company, should have place upon the Journal. Do not begrudge space or time. Upon one occasion the attorney for a company compelled me to enter full and complete deeds of twenty-two pieces of property, that, together with other instruments of writing, covered eighty pages of a large-size Journal, from which I had only two postings to make.

The name of a stockholder or subscriber should not appear upon the General Ledger unless he is a salaried employe, or buys from, or sells to, the company. This latter, however, is forbidden by some companies.

Before a company has been fully organized there may have been more or less outlay in the way of attorney's fees, printing, etc., on part of one or more of the incorporators. When the facts are presented give Mr. Blank individual credit for his outlay (in cash), and treat him as a common creditor, after which, if he demands the amount he expended be deducted from his first installment, give him credit for the full installment paid, and "Contra" charge him through the Cash Book with what appears to be to his credit in the Ledger.

Should the Company donate Stock to one of its officers for a certain service performed, or issue Stock for labor or for anything of no direct value, debit "Working Capital" and credit "Capital Stock" account. *In no case is it a loss* that should be charged to the operating expenses, or is it strictly proper to charge the Expense Account with commissions paid to a broker or agent for selling Stock, while it would be proper to charge Expense with the commission paid for selling the Bonds of the Company.

Upon one occasion, when engaged upon the books of a large corporation, I discovered a large amount of money charged to "Explorations." I inquired of the President the meaning of this seeming singular entry. He replied, "Oh, well, that is all right; pass to the next." I, as I have done on other occasions, "passed to the next."

In connection with this I will give a few entries I have seen made in books, to dispose of transactions, when money has been spent or used around legislative bodies and elsewhere. Two or more of the incorporators that are to be of the directory have been denominated attorneys or agents, whom the Company pay for extra services, but really performed by some unknown third party or parties. This is "charged to Expense Account." Then I have seen a certain number of shares donated to the members who control the Stock, with the understanding the Stock was to be sold as individual property, and the proceeds handed over to parties whose names and transactions dare not go upon the books. Sometimes the Stock is held and the Dividends paid to unknown parties. Then I have seen where Stock has been donated to parties whose habitations are at the bottom of the ocean.

Incorporators naturally look out for themselves. In a long corporation they secure the majority of Stock, either prearranged or by privilege of having the first offer. In a company moderately or fully successful, the profits may be absorbed in paying the salaries of its officers. The small holders may grumble at no dividends; but as the Company does not agree to take back the Stock in case of failure to pay dividends, why all you can do is to grumble, although the laws in some States interfere, and forbid Stockholders voting themselves sinecure places, thus exhausting the profits in drawing the large salaries attached to their positions. A few far-seeing capitalists generally get possession of a valuable Franchise, and capitalize a Company and divide the Stock among themselves. This is termed a Close or a Short Corporation. In a Company of this kind the Stock is always at or above par, with any of it seldom upon the market. A company that absorbs its profits to pay salaries is generally a company carried on "on paper." It is lawful and proper for incorporators, who supply the Assets of a tangible nature for the formation of a company, to allot themselves as many shares as they choose, reserving a certain number to be sold for operating purposes. Their Stock, in common with other Stock sold, is subject to assessment.

There are book-keepers who object to so-called fictitious and nominal accounts. It would be gratifying to learn how the books of some companies could be opened without their aid. They object probably because they have never come in contact with transactions similar to some I have here shown. They being literally some of the

many I have encountered in my experience, I could go further and
give the basis of other organizations; but it would be useless, because
I imagine what I have supplied will, in the hands of competent and
intelligent book-keepers, be sufficient to guide them in commencing
the books of all organizations of peculiar construction. · Shares sold at
par for cash, and entered into the Cash Book, and from there posted
to the credit of Capital Stock account, may be proper enough.
Then the book-keeper who has never stepped beyond the limits of the
"Cash Basis" may be led to argue against fictitious accounts. But
when you have Assets of one sum and another amount of incorporated
Capital; sometimes no Assets; Stock given away and disposed of in
various ways, sold above and below par; the book-keeper is obliged to
adopt a different method than that used in the simple manipulation
of cash. (See Proposition IV, Examples 23 and 24.) In Proposition
I. is a company that is to have a paid-up cash capital. While I could
have debited Cash and credited Capital Stock, and paid no attention
to the Journal, I preferred to introduce the account of Contingencies.
I do this mainly for the purpose of giving a history of the Company's
organization, etc., avoiding the carrying of an account of no value,
but having the appearance of a real debtor, to show from the Capital
Stock account the amount of Stock issued, should it be determined
that fifty per cent. was all that was needed to operate the Company.
Some companies do not issue the Stock to subscribers until all installments are paid. There is no objection to this plan, provided the
installments are for a certainty to be called within a fixed limit. But
a company would find very few, if any, who would be willing to pay
for Stock by installments, and to wait for indefinite period before all
installments would be called. A company runs no risk in issuing the
Stock upon the payment of the first installment, because a subscriber is
lawfully bound to pay all proper demands before he can transfer his
Stock, vote, or draw any Dividends that may be declared.

Should any of those in authority in a Company in which you are
employed endeavor to induce you to make an entry to cover up an
unlawful act, do not let the loss of your place deter your refusal.
Ten thousand times better to sacrifice your position, than be made a
scape-goat or accessory to a crime. If you allow yourself to be made
a tool in one fraudulent transaction, you virtually donate a lien upon
your honor you can never retrieve, while ruin to yourself and disgrace
to those you hold most dear is certain as death. I do not speak of

Joint Stock Companies in general or particularly; but I can recall many instances where men are outcasts and branded as defaulters, who have brought about their condition in their efforts to shield those who have long since deserted them.

Always have your work up before you deposit the books in the safe at the close of the day. By this rule you will have the accounts of all who deal with the house in a proper condition for examination at any time, to the satisfaction of all concerned. Should it be your duty to be cashier as well as book-keeper, *allow no one to meddle with the cash drawer—that is your property until you have to make returns.*

Be independent, but not impudent. A respectful independence wins the admiration of all honorable, high-minded men. Take pride in your work. Never grumble about long hours, or complain that your employer fails to offer you thanks every hour in the day for doing what you have engaged to do. He retains your services, which is proof of his appreciation. Do not be a tattler or inform your employer of every little twaddle among the employes; but go to him at once with anything calculated to injure his interest, no matter who is the offender or what the penalty. Never speak of your employer's peculiarities, even should he in a fit of passion insanely imagine he alone is infallible. Strictly guard the secrets you naturally acquire from your position. You should understand your own place and duties, and endeavor quietly, without intrusion, to understand the place and duties of others. Treat your customers fairly. Never deceive them for the sake af your employer's interest. You may sometime need their influence or financial aid. There are more self-made men who owe their success in life to friends made under these circumstances than to those they have faithfully served. Finally do not imagine what you do not know about book-keeping is not worth knowing; there are lots of that class of fellows.

www.ingramcontent.com/pod-product-compliance
Lightning Source LLC
Chambersburg PA
CBHW021600270326
41931CB00009B/1307